Socialist Explainers: Short answers to big questions

Edited by Elaine Graham-Leigh

COUNTERFIRE

Socialist Explainers:
Short answers to big questions

First published in Great Britain in 2021 by Counterfire,
Bow House, 157 Bow Road, London E3 2SE.
Cover design and layout: Neil Darby

ISBN 978-1-907899-13-3

A catalogue record for this book is available from
the British Library.

Printed and bound in Great Britain.
www.counterfire.org

Contents

Introduction

Why do we need socialist theory?
Dominic Alexander

We live in a world where capitalist ideas are dominant. This is not just a matter of establishment propaganda, but of everyday experience, in which capitalism appears to be the natural way of things. To paraphrase Marx, the thoughts of the ruling class are ruling thoughts. The way society works creates a sort of common sense which reinforces the normality in which profit making drives everything, and the social structures which enable the exploiting class are not questionable.

Yet, nothing is monolithic, and most people's experience teaches them that much is wrong with the system, that obvious injustice and inhumanity are rife. In order to survive, working people need to rely on co-operation, and shared values of equity, at least. Meanwhile, the system produces a vast range of problems, and outright crises, which require sacrifices from the great mass of people, while the ruling class is protected in its wealth and power. This was true in the early years of the industrial revolution, and it still is now.

Capitalism, however stable it has been at some points in its history, therefore always creates experiences which drive many people to criticise and even reject the naturalness of the system, and the assumptions that go along with it. On our own, nonetheless, we are likely to doubt our misgivings about the way the world works, and it is difficult to contradict the weight of established opinion, let alone challenge the structures imposed upon us.

This can only be done collectively; when working people organise together, ideas and activity can be developed that point to alternatives to capitalism. People come to understand that they occupy a particular position in society; they belong to the working class with interests opposed to the exploiters, the bourgeoisie or capitalist class. It is out of all this practice and understanding that socialist movements develop.

Socialist theory aims to look behind the common-sense appearances of the economy, the state and society in general to understand the reality of things. It becomes apparent that in the contradictions and crises of capitalism, there lies the possibility of a different society altogether. Economics does not work as the apologists for capitalism insist it does, and Marx was not the first to take up economic analysis from the standpoint of the working class. Since him, many radicals have built upon his work.

Far from capitalism being the best system to produce and distribute goods, or the only one, it has been shown that the system always tends towards crisis, and produces vast wealth for a few, amid unnecessary poverty and struggle for most of the world's population. It also creates a continual series of devastating wars, through the imperialist competition between capitalist states.

Similarly, racism and sexism are not natural or inevitable in any society, but are deeply rooted in the structures that capitalism historically inherited, transformed and continues to develop to reproduce itself. Other problems created by capitalism, like environmental crises, tend to be blamed on the inherent greed of human beings, but these too can be shown to be the product of capitalism's drive for profit against any other consideration.

Socialist theory has grown for over two hundred years through the work of activists developing analysis, strategy and organisation. Theory is needed to lay bare the real workings of capitalism, and the most effective ways of organising people to oppose and overthrow that system of exploitation and oppression. It is the result of the collective effort and experience of the working class, and, despite inevitable controversies and disagreements, we cannot act effectively without all this endeavour.

At its best, socialist theory enables successful organisation, which itself fuels wider and deeper understanding of capitalism and the alternatives. As Marx famously said, 'philosophers have hitherto only interpreted the world in various ways; the point is to change it.'

Section 1: Socialist basics

What is socialism?

Chris Nineham

Socialism is the idea that working people should organise society collectively and democratically in the interests of the majority. It is based on two insights about the modern world. One, that we can produce enough to satisfy everyone's needs. Two, that working people, the overwhelming majority around the globe, have an interest and ability to create a world that is fair, sustainable, and free of all oppression and coercion.

The idea arose in the nineteenth century after it became clear that despite the egalitarian ideas of the French Revolution, emerging industrial capitalism was based on the brutal exploitation of working people by a tiny elite. Capitalism brought unimaginable wealth for a few but misery and poverty for the majority.

At first socialism took the form of utopian plans imagined by visionary individuals. As capitalism developed, working people built their own organisations, raised their own demands and began to struggle for radical change. In Britain, the Chartists fought for the vote from the 1830s to try and secure a society based on equality, the nationalisation of industry and land, and free education for all.

Marx and Engels built on this experience and that of the great capitalist revolutions (the Dutch and the English in the seventeenth century, and the American and French at the end of the eighteenth century). They argued that it would take popular uprisings to dismantle capitalism and create an equal, free society. For them a revolutionary movement was necessary not just to overcome the capitalists' resistance to change but also to prepare people for a new society. Socialism had to be participatory: 'The emancipation of the working class is the act of the working class.' The Paris Commune of 1871 bore this out. For over two months the working people of Paris took over their city and ran it themselves with new, highly democratic institutions in which women played a leading role.

The carnage of the First World War caused a deep crisis and helped generate mass socialist movements across Europe and around the world from Mexico to China. Workers took power in Russia for the first time in 1917. In Germany, a revolution brought down the monarchy and workers' councils sprung up around Europe.

Tragically, the revolutionary upsurge after the First World War was contained and defeated. After missed opportunities in the West, fascist governments crushed working-class movements in Italy, Spain and Germany. In Russia, Stalin destroyed the revolution, dismantled workers' democracy and imposed a state-capitalist order.

Socialism however has remained the great aspiration of working people. Over the last hundred years there have been scores of workers' uprisings around the world and left-wing governments have been elected in country after country. Many of these governments have made important changes: introducing welfare states, free education and childcare services, health provision and so on, making life more bearable for working people. But nowhere have they been able to deal with the central issue that capitalist production is run for profit by a handful of big corporations, with all the inequality, suffering and environmental chaos that involves.

Socialism means turning the world upside down. It means working people taking control to liberate humanity not just from poverty and hunger but from the misery of forced labour in the factories and offices of the big corporations. It means bringing to an end the horrors of war and competition between nations. It means overturning sexual oppression and destroying the virus of racism. It means unleashing the creativity of ordinary people to solve the world's problems and build a sustainable society in which we can all express ourselves and flourish. It means turning into reality Marx's famous phrase that 'the liberation of one is dependent on the liberation of all.' It will only be achieved by the active mobilisation of millions.

Does human nature make socialism impossible?

Lucy Nichols

The idea that humans are selfish and greedy is often used to try to discredit socialists. The right claims that human nature renders socialism an impossible, utopian dream.

The argument runs that because we are all selfish, it is only natural that we live under an economic system in which 'greed is good'. The contention is that free-market capitalism is an expression of human nature: self-interest rules and humans must compete in the market to meet their needs. Two other conclusions follow. One, that there needs to be a strong central authority to hold our egotistical behaviour in check. Two, that any attempt at collectivism is doomed by our selfishness.

There are many indications that these assumptions are false and that people often act with kindness and cooperation. Take the coronavirus crisis. During the pandemic, nurses and doctors and other workers put their lives at risk despite poor working conditions, low pay, and lack of PPE. Mutual aid groups sprang up to support the most vulnerable. Millions have shown support for key workers. Despite all the difficulties, the majority of people observed successive lockdowns, very often not simply out of self-interest, but to protect others and wider society.

Even in 'normal' times, millions of people work in the NHS, social services and other parts of the welfare state on low pay, often because they want to improve the lives and conditions of others. Particularly at times of popular struggle, there are fantastic acts of solidarity and self-sacrifice. In summer 2020, millions of people around the world from all races and backgrounds came out to protest against police violence in support of the US Black Lives Matter movement.

Given this potential, how come the world remains so unequal and competitive? The mainstream, capitalist explanation is that we are born unequal: some of us possess talents that others do not, some of us are lazy and others are hardworking. This - paired with the idea that we are also naturally selfish – explains deep-seated inequality.

Socialists argue that actually, things work the other way around. Humans have the capacity to behave in different ways and, more than anything, our behaviour is shaped by the society in which we live. It is the way that capitalism is organised that encourages people to 'look after number one'. The capitalists themselves ruthlessly exploit working people for their own profit and are in constant competition with each other. The rest of the population have no choice but to compete for jobs, for housing and services, and to buy shoddy goods produced for profit by the big corporations. All this is backed up by an education and media that constantly reproduce the idea that it is self-interest that drives society.

There is another side to our experience under capitalism. The existence of trade unions and left-wing parties, struggles for better wages, for health and safety at work, or for better services and benefits, all show that working people know that there is such a thing as society. Working people regularly push back against exploitation and want society to be fairer and more collective.

Collectivity is at its most intense when great struggles break out, whether against racism or austerity or job cuts. In these circumstances human solidarity comes to the fore, ideas of competition start to break down, and people focus their energies on trying to force change that will very often benefit all working people. At these moments it becomes clear that humanity's defining nature is our ability collectively to change the world.

Why does class matter?

David McAllister

Oxfam reported in 2019 that the richest 26 individuals possess the same wealth as the poorest 50% of the human race. This stark statistic points to the most fundamental division in society, that between the super-rich and the majority. Understanding it is central to grasping how society works. It is also vital to understanding how it could be transformed.

Mainstream discussions of class often focus on lifestyle or culture; whether someone owns a house, where they live, or even their dress sense or diet. While these things can be pointers, they don't get us very far. Even income doesn't get to the bottom of how class actually operates and shapes society.

Capitalism is based on production for profit. This profit goes into the hands of a tiny minority of people who own and run business, whether it's a software company, a supermarket chain, a hotel business, or an arms company. These are the capitalists proper, modern members of what Marx and Engels called the bourgeoisie. As they accumulate huge levels of wealth, they are backed by the power of state institutions which, by and large, govern in their interests.

Then there is the class which has nothing to sell but their labour: their work. Nowadays, workers are the overwhelming majority around the world. Workers are exploited by capitalists, because the wages they earn are a fraction of the wealth the capitalist pockets from production. Other classes in society, the middle class say, or an independent peasantry in some countries, fit in different ways into an economy driven relentlessly by this central process, the extraction of profit from working people by big business.

Which class you belong to, therefore, is defined by your relationship to the means of production: how you fit into the system of production and distribution. The nature of the work changes over time. Marx and Engels' time was marked by the growth of heavy manual industry, including mills, shipyards and mines. The decline in manufacturing in Britain means that white-collar and service work is now a more common experience.

This has led some commentators to suggest that the working class has actually disappeared. But class is a social relationship, centred around the production of goods, services and wealth. As such, exploitation remains the reality, whether it happens in a coal mine or a supermarket.

This relationship between the two classes brings us to the class struggle. The capitalists are locked into competition with each other to make as much profit as possible. Workers have an interest in the opposite; in clinging on to as much as possible of the value of what they produce. This puts workers in a unique position in society. Capitalists are dependent upon workers for profit, and workers form the overwhelming majority in society. If they can overcome internal divisions by challenging all forms of oppression, workers have tremendous power. When they take strike action, they can bring the central drive of the system to a halt.

In Britain, it has been some time since we saw mass resistance in the workplaces. British politics over the last forty years has been marked by a relentless assault on the working class and its organisations. However, neoliberal capitalism has also led to a growing feeling that the system is rigged against working people. One product of this has been a sharp increase in street protests, particularly in the last twenty years. This sense of anger and injustice also found expression in Jeremy Corbyn's leadership of the

Labour Party, with its central slogan 'for the many, not the few'. When this accumulated anger is connected to organisation at the point of production, the result can be explosive.

This is why class remains so fundamental. It is not just a benign way of categorising people. In essence, class is really a description of how society is actually run. Without a firm grasp of this, there cannot be any serious understanding of capitalism and the fight against it.

What went wrong in Russia?

Vladimir Unkovski-Korica

For much of the twentieth century, the Soviet Union was a byword for the alternative to capitalism. Its disappearance has helped to delegitimise the notion of radical change ever since. Yet the Soviet Union was not what it seemed. It maintained the aura of a revolutionary state because it was born out of one of the greatest revolutions of the modern world.

In 1917, workers and soldiers toppled the Romanov dynasty, which had ruled for three centuries, and formed soviets, or councils; highly democratic representative organs of power built from the workplace up. Initially, the soviets shared power with sections of the old order, but compromise became impossible. By November 1917, workers had elected the revolutionary Bolsheviks into these councils with the slogan: 'All power to the Soviets!'

It did not stop there. Workers across the world looked to Soviet Russia for inspiration. Through strikes and demonstrations, they tried to stop their countries helping the counter-revolutionary armies in the Russian Civil War, which the Bolsheviks won by 1921. However, attempts at establishing soviet republics were repeatedly quashed militarily, from Hungary and Bavaria in the aftermath of the First World War, to Shanghai in 1927.

The Soviet Union, as the country was known from 1922, stood isolated and surrounded by hostile powers. Soon, a quiet counter-revolution occurred. Without a formal change of regime, the state departed from any notion of working-class democracy and moved to accelerate autarkic economic development at the expense of the population.

It quashed opposition to this move led by Leon Trotsky, co-leader of the Bolsheviks in 1917, who hoped to revive soviet democracy and international revolution. Democracy in the soviets had already died a slow and silent death in the period of the civil war, as a state bureaucracy had arisen to run nationalised industry.

Although the Bolsheviks had remained wedded to protecting working-class living standards and spreading revolution, a powerful section of the party and state bureaucracy, led by Joseph Stalin, now argued that the Soviet Union could only survive if it industrialised quickly. In Stalin's words: 'We are fifty or a hundred years behind the advanced countries. We must make up this gap in ten years. Either we do it or they will crush us.'

Because state leaders continued to profess their commitment to socialism, and to aid communist parties abroad when it suited their interests, the Soviet Union continued to command the loyalty of millions of working-class militants for decades.

The reality, however, was that it had become a bureaucratic state-capitalist regime. The state held the commanding role in economic affairs, but production was no longer about serving working-class needs. Instead, it was about preparing for war. Even as economic growth under the famous five-year plans rocketed in the 1930s, working-class living standards fell and millions in the countryside died of starvation.

Geopolitical competition, first against Nazi Germany in the Second World War, then the United States in the Cold War, shaped the Soviet economy for decades. It scored major successes: the T34 tank was better than its Nazi German counterparts and the Soviet Union reached parity in nuclear missiles with the USA in the 1970s. But by this time, it was spending a fifth of its GDP on the military.

This meant that external priorities decisively shaped Soviet economic policies, at the expense of its population, which did nothing to defend the state as it crumbled in the late 1980s and early 1990s. Building 'socialism in one country' as Stalin had promised to do proved not just impossible but turned the Soviet Union into the opposite.

If we wish to build socialism in the twenty-first century, we have to remain committed to the democratic and internationalist vision of 1917.

Is a society without oppression possible?
Elaine Graham-Leigh

Discussions of oppression sometimes give the impression that it's inevitable. These see oppression as arising from human nature. In this view, individuals are predisposed to be sexist, racist and so on by tendencies that have their roots deep in human biology and prehistory. This would mean that it would be difficult or even impossible to overcome these inherent traits even in the most progressive society. Clearly this is a depressing conclusion, but is it right?

The history of oppression shows us that in fact, there have been complex human societies which did manage to be genuinely egalitarian. There are examples from all over the world, from Aboriginal Australia, to prehistoric Turkey, the Indus Valley and North America before European colonisation. What these examples all have in common is that not only did they not have oppression, they did not have exploitation either. They weren't class societies.

This was a key insight of Frederick Engels, in *The Origin of the Family, Private Property and the State*. Engels traced the origin of women's oppression – the earliest form of oppression – to the development of class. In a free society, there would be no need for men as a group to try to control women as a group. If, though, some men have started to build up their own private property, the only way they could be sure of passing it on to their own children would be if they controlled the women with whom they had those children. This was, Engels realised, how women were themselves made into property.

Women's oppression therefore developed because it

served the interests of the earliest ruling class. As well as allowing ruling-class men to control their own property, it also protected ruling-class power by giving lower-class men a stake in the class system. The lower-class men might themselves be exploited, but at least they could lord it over their women.

Other oppressions have developed for similar reasons. Racism can feel so engrained in our society that it's difficult to imagine that we have ever been without it. In fact, people in the ancient and medieval world weren't generally that bothered about skin colour. Oppression on this basis was only encouraged by the elites in the early modern period to justify the slave trade.

Other forms of prejudice, such as antisemitism, did exist in the Middle Ages, but even there, its development was encouraged by the ruling class. Pogroms against Jewish communities in medieval Europe were often blamed on the mob, but were almost always driven by people of higher social class.

In the same way again, we can see that homophobia is encouraged to develop in periods when the nuclear family is seen as key to ensuring a continuing supply of exploitable workers. When the ruling class takes this view, then people in gay or lesbian relationships can appear as a threat. At other times, they can look more like a potential market with high disposable incomes, so homophobia will start to be officially frowned upon.

What this history shows is that oppression does not arise from human nature. It is, rather, part of the developing way in which the ruling class maintains its power in a class society. It is certainly possible to have a society without oppression; many people in our history have lived in such societies. What isn't possible is to eradicate oppression without also overthrowing the class system that it was developed to serve.

Will racism always be with us?

Yonas Makoni

Martin Luther King once said that 'the arc of the moral universe is long, but it bends toward justice.' This unqualified optimism about the possibility of eradicating racism seems hard to fathom today. The refrain 'nothing has changed' has become increasingly common within the anti-racist movement, reflecting widespread frustration and anger over the lack of progress on racial disparities.

While such statements are useful in some instances, they can also lead to an unproductive pessimism, to the belief that nothing has changed because nothing can change. In order to rekindle MLK's sense of optimism, it might be useful to ask where racism actually comes from and what that means for the fight against it.

The difference between socialists and liberals on racism can be, in many ways, boiled down to the question of from where racism comes. For liberals, racism is defined primarily as an aggregate of bad or misinformed opinions, attitudes or biases. Tackling racism is, as such, primarily a matter of changing minds through education or social pressure. Similar to charity fundraising or individualised approaches to combating climate change, this conception believes in stimulating fundamental change by making people feel bad. Not for nothing, it usually leads to pessimism.

For socialists, racism comes from the top, from the seats of power. If racism persists, this is because the institutional structures that produce it still exist. Just as with climate change, this conception allows us to understand that, while individual beliefs and habits are important and certainly should change, they are not the determining factor.

Those in power do not promote racism out of malice, but because the logic of the system they are upholding drives them to it. The needs of competition drives capitalists, on the one hand, to incessantly intensify the exploitation of the workforce and to seek new opportunities for profiteering, triggering working-class resistance.

Politicians, on the other hand, are tasked with promoting this capitalist expansion, while containing its destabilising effect. A series of constraints force politicians into this dilemma. Firstly, since the state functions to maintain social stability, it must avoid economic crises by all means and convince capitalists that the country is a safe place to do business. Secondly, capitalist interests positively shape policy in numerous ways: through lobbying, candidate selection, media pressure and so on.

Racism provides a clever way out here. Firstly, it allows capitalists to intensify their exploitation of the working class without undermining social stability, since it pits one group of workers against another. Institutional racism thus forces ethnic minorities and migrants into precarity, forcing them into jobs with much lower pay and worse conditions. But this super-exploitation of minorities also creates a downward pressure on the standards and bargaining power of the working class as a whole.

On the other hand, it also allows politicians to reconcile this protection of capitalist interests with their task of maintaining national cohesion. Particularly in times of crisis, it allows them to sustain cross-class, political coalitions by redirecting popular anger towards minorities, scapegoating them for society's hardships.

But to focus only on why and how racism works is one-sided, because it neglects the countervailing forces. In its tendency to intensify the exploitation of all workers, capitalism not only divides the working class but also creates a basis for class unity. As we can see from the history of anti-racist and working-class movements, there have been many times in which racist division has been overcome and workers have learnt the necessity of unity in pursuit of their common interests. However, to succeed in the long term, these movements must transform the economic and political structures that seek to divide them.

By isolating the role that racism plays in the economic and political context, we treat it as something that is historically situated and therefore not eternal. If it is not eternal, it can be overcome. But it also rules out half measures. To defeat racism, we need to also defeat the forces that rely on it.

Section 2: How capitalism works, and doesn't

Is capitalism in decline?

Dominic Alexander

Capitalism globally has not recovered from the crash of 2008. We have since been living through a period of persistent low growth that qualifies as a new 'long depression' to rival the profound crises of the late nineteenth century and the 1930s. In every previous crisis, capitalism has recovered, and entered into a new phase of profitability and expansion. The question remains whether, and how, it might do so again, or has capitalism as a system reached the end of its historical capacity to renew itself?

A major mechanism by which crisis has been overcome is through a wave of new technologies, which cheapen production, allow the expansion of new industries, and restore the rate of profit. Always such booms, however, contain the seeds of the next major crisis, since when new technology has been generalised across the economy, average profitability once again declines. New methods of production generally reduce the quantity of labour needed to manufacture commodities. Initially this can raise profitability for some industries at least, and if the cost of the reproduction of labour is cheapened, for example through cheaper food, this can raise profitability generally. However, labour is the source of surplus value, and hence profit, so the less labour involved, the less surplus value is produced. As a result, the long-term trend eventually re-asserts itself, and the overall rate of profit in the economy is reduced. Crisis resumes.

The economic history of the last fifty years suggests that escaping from crisis is becoming more difficult for the system than was historically the case. Various studies, using different methods, have all shown that profit rates broadly declined in the late 60s and early 70s. They recovered only slightly as neoliberal policies from the late 1970s cut public services, and restructured production globally, driving down wages and costs of production. Profit rates then resumed a downward trend, again declining before the crash of 2008, and remaining historically low. The latest crisis therefore comes after a long period in which capitalism had failed to re-capture the high growth rates of the post-war boom.

The current wave of innovation in computing and digital technology has been underway for some time, and has indeed given rise to huge new corporations, and billionaire capitalists. However important this sector has been for the last three decades, it has not translated into a convincing renewal of capitalist growth and profitability more generally. Capitalism requires ever greater expansion, but lately it appears to be running only to stand still.

Tellingly, notable successes such as Google and Facebook are engaged not in commodity production as such, but rely upon advertising as sources of revenue. That is to say, they are taking a slice of existing surplus value, not creating new value themselves from production. Yet capitalism depends upon value creating activity. As a vector for renewing capitalism, such successes look barren. What we are seeing now is a far cry from the electronics, chemical and automation booms of the late nineteenth and early twentieth centuries.

Who is to say that some other wave of productive innovation is not about to arrive? It may be, or it may be that capitalism is approaching a limit to its ability to cheapen production in ways that allow for accelerated expansion. Moreover, there is nowhere significant in the world for capitalism to expand into; China is clearly part of the world system. The top-heavy growth of the financial sphere, and its absurdities, is a sign that capital is fleeing from productive activity into competition over the share of existing social surplus.

Another sign of the same problem is that housing is now a sink for unproductive capital, actually creating a greater drag for the system as a whole as this increases the cost of the reproduction of labour. These and other such problems suggest that capitalism is becoming, even in its most prosperous zones, dysfunctional by its own low standards. None of this is even to mention accelerating, and multiple, ecological crises.

Another way that capitalism has, in the past, restored profitability is through the massive destruction of rival capitals. This happened in the Second World War, for example, and was a major basis for the post-war boom. Capitalism might be in decline, but it is capable of unthinkable levels of devastation in its desperation for the renewal of profitability.

We cannot wait to find out if capitalism has reached its own internal limits, we must organise to replace it, before it destroys us all in its death-throes.

Why is the labour theory of value so important?

Dominic Alexander

We live in a global society suffering from colossal extremes of wealth and poverty. Throughout the world, millionaires and billionaires maintain that they deserve their riches because their business activities create the wealth. When such claims come from hedge-fund managers shorting stocks on the market, they ring hollow to most people. On the other hand, the idea that manufacturers and 'productive' businesses create something of worth has greater traction.

Yet, it is not true: the only creators of surplus in the economy are those who do the work, and this sector represents the great mass of ordinary people who actually make society function. It is labour that is the source of all surplus value. That is to say, all the profit that is appropriated by the capitalist class, and its servants in the managing structures of economy and society, comes from the labour of working people.

Back at the origins of modern economic theory, political economists were all very concerned with the problem of 'value'; its origins and how it came to be distributed in the way it was. Their conclusions started to trouble bourgeois society, as they began to reveal the real working of capitalism, and the profession soon turned away altogether from questions of value. As a result, even many left-wing economists today continue to reject the concept of value.

It was, however, a pro-capitalist economist, David Ricardo (1772-1823), who, drawing upon his predecessors, created the first 'labour theory of value'. Marx took over from Ricardo, making some crucial revisions of the theory, and using it to create his uncompromising critique of the capitalist system. This is why so few modern economists dare to touch this whole question: the answers lead in the wrong direction for them.

The standard assumption is that 'supply and demand' determine price, but as Marx pointed out, when those two factors are balanced, then they explain nothing. The mainstream fallback position is to say that the price of a product is derived from a combination of the value of raw materials, capital investment and labour. The conclusion is then that workers receive a fair recompense for their work based on the exchange-value of labour 'in the marketplace'.

Marx showed why this eclectic approach also explained nothing, and how the exploitation of workers is, in fact, hidden by a focus on the workings of supply and demand in the 'free market'. Neither the input of raw materials nor capital into a product can explain the origin of surplus value, from which capitalist profit is derived. Both represent 'dead labour'. The former is from the work that has been done to turn natural resources into exchangeable commodities, and the latter being an accumulation of surplus derived from labour that is stored as capital. Neither can produce a surplus above the value of their own inputs.

Only human labour can produce such a surplus. That is to say that unlike all the other inputs into a commodity, only human labour power can produce more value than it requires, on average in society, to maintain the supply of productive workers. All that the capitalist can put into a commodity is the fixed value of the capital and commodities that have already been produced. Labour power is 'variable', in Marx's terms, because more value can be forced out of a worker than she needs to be paid, according to the price of labour power in the market. This 'surplus value' is appropriated by the capitalist, who, if successful in selling commodities on the market, realises the surplus as profit.

This is why capitalism is always an exploitative system, even when it appears on the surface that workers are receiving a 'fair' wage according to the market price of labour. Some capitalists can receive more than their share of the total surplus value in the economy through market competition, or access to political power, for example, but at the level of society as a whole, these variations all cancel out. So, however the total social surplus gets distributed among particular capitalists, it is all derived ultimately from paying workers less than the total value of what they have produced through their labour.

Capital is no more than accumulated surplus value derived from the difference between the workforce's capacity for labour, and the social cost of maintaining that workforce. The claims that it is the owners of capital who themselves produce social wealth are wholly baseless. Their demands that spending on social goods, from housing to health care, must be limited so as not to place too great a burden on 'wealth creators' are therefore entirely bogus. The argument represents a reversal of the truth. It is profit that seeks to crowd out the share of the social surplus that goes to the reproduction of human life. It is only the elimination of capitalist profit-making that can enable society to prosper.

Why does the rate of profit matter?

Dominic Alexander

Marx's theory that capitalism shows a tendency over the long term for the rate of profit to fall has been much misunderstood, and lately often dismissed or abandoned. It remains, nonetheless, an essential part of any Marxist analysis of how capitalism creates instability, crisis and destruction. Historically, the decline of the rate of profit can be shown to have happened, but there are also counteracting forces and events which allow it to recover temporarily. The tendency for profit rates to decline does not mean that capitalism is likely to collapse by itself, but it does mean that it has a drive towards crisis which is increasingly destructive of society and the environment.

The decline of the rate of profit is rooted in one of capitalism's central motors: the accumulation of new technology and machinery in order to produce more commodities, more cheaply and quickly. Capitalists are driven to this by the need to compete with each other for profits, so this is a broadly constant pressure on production, although in practice it results in waves of new technology cascading through economies in historical phases.

The problem for profitability is that profit itself only comes from the exploitation of labour: from the difference between the value of the wage paid to the worker, and the value of the commodity produced by labour power. The difference is called 'surplus value' by Marx, and this is realised into actual profit through selling commodities on the market.

The problem for the rate of profit is that surplus value only comes from 'living' labour. It does not come from raw materials, or machinery, or the marketing of products, it only comes from the additional labour required to create a new commodity from those fixed costs. One capitalist may undercut another through use of more advanced technology, and less labour, and so individually realise a higher profit rate. As every capitalist, through competition, is forced to adopt the same technology, the proportion of surplus value being created to total capital begins to fall (the total *mass* of profit can still be growing greater). Over time, it takes more capital investment on average to produce the same level of profit as before; the rate of profit falls as a result of the accumulation of technology.

There are many ways in which this tendency can be reversed. For example, new technology which cheapens the cost of living allows wages to be proportionally reduced, pushing up the rate of profit. There are a range of such countervailing factors, but they always do, over time, come to be neutralised by the central tendency for the rise in proportion of capital investment against labour to depress profitability. Periodic major crises are the result of this tendency, from the Long Depression of 1873 to the 1890s, the Great Depression of the 1930s, the crisis of the 1970s to today's since 2008.

There is another highly disturbing way in which profit rates can be restored, and this is through the wholesale destruction of one block of capital interests by another block. This was what occurred during the Second World War, which finally ended the Great Depression, and laid the basis for the post-war boom. Humanity cannot afford for capitalism to solve a crisis this way again, but crises in profitability underpin the conflicts between imperialist powers which lead to that kind of catastrophe.

The tendency for the rate of profit to fall means that capitalism descends into destructive crisis as a matter of course. It does not mean that capitalism will fall apart of its own accord, at least not without potentially destroying the world along with it. It does mean that capitalism cannot be stabilised for long, and that socialists must organise and fight to replace it.

Can state spending avert crises?

Dominic Alexander

Capitalism is an unstable system that has always produced crisis. It was in the very first commercial capitalist state, the Dutch Republic in 1636-7, that the first such crisis occurred. This was the Tulip mania where speculation over tulip-bulb prices caused a financial bubble that, on bursting, precipitated an economic slump. A system dominated by the search for profit, rather than production for social need, will create crises as a matter of course.

Mainstream economics has always claimed that capitalism produces a balance, or 'equilibrium', and that crisis is the result of 'outside shocks', such as government policies that interfere with profit-making. History tells us otherwise. Throughout the height of the industrial revolution in Britain there were frequent, devastating crises. This was even before the first structural world crisis of capitalism hit in the 1870s, in a long downturn that did not end until the late 1890s.

Imperialist expansion, including arms spending that culminated in the First World War, did much to bring capitalism back to prosperity. The next structural crisis was the Great Depression of the 1930s, which again was not truly ended until massive investment in arms took off at the start of the Second World War.

Capitalism in the 1930s was discredited in the eyes of a great many people across the world, and a solution needed to be found to make the system acceptable once again. The orthodoxy that governments should not interfere in the economy, the doctrine of *laissez-faire* or free markets, was largely abandoned in favour of government intervention of one kind or another. The key figure in the new economics was John Maynard Keynes, who argued that the central problem of capitalism was the lack of sufficient demand to encourage capitalists to invest in the expectation of profit.

Keynes argued that crisis could be ended, or even forestalled, if governments invested in the economy, it didn't really matter how, to create more demand. Capitalists would recover confidence that profits could be made as a result of there being more demand, and so would invest. More goods would be made, more people would have jobs, and money to spend on those goods. The government would recover the money it had spent as the economy roared back to life.

There are many examples from the 1930s of government spending improving the lives of people, notably from President Franklin Delano Roosevelt's 'New Deal' in the USA. Nonetheless, the Great Depression didn't really end until government spending on the war reached far greater proportions than was spent on peacetime welfare, infrastructure and job creation beforehand. This kind of investment is capital intensive, and highly profitable, in contrast to the pure expenses of health care or education.

The Keynesian promise that government spending would have a 'multiplier effect' on the rest of the economy proved to be if not illusory, then at least quite weak in impact in peacetime conditions. The extreme conditions of state direction of the wartime economy would never be tolerated by capital under normal circumstances.

There is a reason for the weakness of the 'multiplier effect'. It is because the system is not driven by a simple matter of consumer demand as Keynesians think. Instead, what matters is the search for high profit rates by capitalists. Capitalists require high returns on their investments not simply out of greed, but by the need to survive competition with each other. Profitability comes first, always.

Profit ultimately comes from paying workers a wage that is less than the value that their labour has created. It does not come from the play of supply and demand in the marketplace, as Keynesian economics assumes. Therefore, stimulating demand does not automatically bring about the conditions that will restore profitability, and hence growth, to the economy. In truth, one major way that capital can restore profitability is to increase the exploitation of workers, by cutting wages, raising hours, and increasing the intensity of work; all conditions that capital can impose more easily on labour during conditions of war, or high unemployment, for example.

The extreme levels of capital destruction during the Second World War led to a post-war situation where investment was highly profitable, and capital was willing to tolerate rising wages and measures of social welfare. These were the circumstances in which Keynesian 'demand management' policies appeared to be successful, but they depended upon a period of high profit rates. Once these began to fall, a new crisis developed in the 1970s. Consequently, government spending came under attack by the forces of capital, seeing it as a rival to its search for a greater share of the social surplus from which profit is taken.

Government spending on its own does not solve capitalist crisis, which stems not simply from a lack of demand, but ultimately from falling profit rates. This does not mean that socialists should not argue for the right *kind* of government spending; government investment in socially useful measures, such as health, education, and ecological sustainability, all remain vitally important for their own sakes. Capitalism needs to be forced to solve a crisis through its own resources, not through the exploitation and degradation of society.

Nonetheless, socially useful government spending will not end an economic crisis within the capitalist system. What it can do, if there is sufficient mass struggle to force the right measures to be taken, is to start to provide a bridge into a different type of economy altogether. The only solution in the longer view is to build a system that is not driven by the tyranny of profit rates, but by social and ecological need.

What is imperialism?

Dragan Plavšić

The best way of getting a handle on imperialism is to get a handle on how capitalism works.

Capitalism is a ruthlessly competitive system. Competition defines its essential character. From banks to oil corporations, from supermarkets to car manufacturers, a permanent 'war of all against all' is being fought for market share. But competition is never just economic. Corporations weaponise every means at their disposal – for example, by currying favour with politicians - in order to outdo competitors at whose hands they otherwise risk rack and ruin.

Indeed, competition must by its very nature have winners and losers, producing intensely uneven results. Some corporations come out on top while others go to the wall. Some people accumulate wealth while others lose their jobs. Some areas of a country prosper while others stagnate or decline. Extreme unevenness is inevitable in a system based on competition.

Capitalism first took secure hold in Britain before going global. And when competition went global, the weaponising of every available means to overcome foreign competitors in conditions of extreme unevenness also went global, giving rise to imperialism.

As nationally successful corporations outgrew domestic limits and sought markets and resources abroad to enhance competitiveness, states weaponised the economic, political but especially the military means at their disposal to provide corporations with the decisive advantages needed to outstrip their competitors from other states. Thus, the competition that characterised relations between corporations within states came to characterise relations between states.

The extreme unevenness afflicting national economies now afflicted the global economy. Some economies dominated world markets while others struggled to make ends meet. And the stronger the economy, the greater the political and military power of a state to project itself beyond national limits.

The result was a hierarchy of states ranked by their concentrated economic, political and military weight. The states at the apex of this hierarchy were 'imperialist' as they possessed the power to dominate weaker states across the globe, if necessary, by force. But hierarchies based on competition sit on treacherously shifting sands. As one global imperialism rises, it must do so at the expense of another. As a result, their struggles have world-destructive consequences for us all.

Thus, Britain was the foremost imperialist state of the nineteenth century, exercising its power by colonising large parts of the globe. By the turn of the century, however, it was challenged by Germany, with the ensuing struggle between them decided by the horrendous slaughter of the First and Second World Wars.

By 1945, with Britain exhausted and Germany defeated, the US emerged as the leading imperialist power. Opposed by Russia, an imperialist power based on a type of state capitalism, their Cold War brought us to the very brink of nuclear self-annihilation.

The US won the Cold War, since when it has been the supreme imperialist state. But today it is under challenge from the emerging imperialist power of China. As a result, the prospect of a new and terrifying Cold War now looms over us.

If there is to be an effective political response to this from the left, a clear and determined focus on opposing our own imperialism will be essential. The UK is a key partner of the US. Mass protests can thwart the UK's plans to support the US, and also weaken the alliance between them.

The main enemy is at home, therefore. This principle has guided the campaigning work of the Stop the War Coalition (the mass demonstration it organised in 2003 came close to preventing the UK's participation in the Iraq war). It should guide anti-war activists in imperialist states everywhere.

Why is Palestine important?

Alex Snowdon

Israel was established in 1948 through the ethnic cleansing of the Palestinians on a massive scale. At least 700,000 Palestinians were forced off their own land. They were removed to make way for a new state that explicitly privileged the rights of one group (Jews) over those of another (the indigenous Palestinian Arabs). Israel was created as an ethnocracy – an apartheid state – characterised by a regime of Jewish supremacy. This was the *Nakba*; Arabic for catastrophe.

At a time of widespread decolonisation – with, most famously, India gaining independence in 1947 – Israel was a new settler-colonial state. Zionism was a movement, emerging in the late nineteenth century, that focused on Jewish settlement in historic Palestine, with a view to it becoming a national home for Jews. It was, according to the Zionists, a land without a people for a people without a land.

Zionism was one response to widespread antisemitism in Europe. That antisemitism reached its horrifying climax in the Holocaust, which galvanised international support for the Zionist project. However, Palestine was not a land without a people. Rather than being the desert of Zionist imagination, it was a cosmopolitan society with a substantial Palestinian population.

Zionist terror gangs killed Palestinians and forced huge numbers out of their homes during 1947-9. The result was a state that treated those Palestinians who remained inside Israel's borders as second-class citizens. Palestinians outside Israel became the world's largest refugee community. In 1967 Israel further expanded its territory, annexing east Jerusalem and occupying Gaza and the West Bank, bringing large numbers of Palestinians under its military rule.

Israel has always required Western imperialist backing. In 1917, Zionist ambitions were boosted by the Balfour Declaration, which pledged Britain's support for the aspiration to a Jewish national home. Jewish settlement in Palestine grew under the British Mandate after World War One. Once Israel was established, it was the US that became the primary imperial sponsor, especially from the 1960s onwards, with vast sums of military aid. The US increasingly saw Israel as a crucial strategic ally in the Middle East.

The Oslo 'peace process' of the 1990s did nothing to redress the historic injustices faced by the Palestinians. It entrenched the idea that Palestinians could only aspire to a separate state occupying a fraction of historic Palestine, while Israel greatly expanded its settlements in the occupied West Bank. It had nothing to offer the Palestinians suffering inequality and discrimination inside Israel and was silent on the Palestinian refugees (or their right of return) exiled outside of Palestine altogether.

Today's reality is a system of apartheid. There is, in truth, a single apartheid state stretching from the Mediterranean Sea to the River Jordan. Israel controls all this territory and subjects Palestinians to oppression that varies in form: Palestinians in Israel are second-class and often impoverished citizens, Palestinians in the West Bank endure military rule, Palestinians in east Jerusalem are squeezed out by evictions, demolitions and institutional hostility, and Palestinians in Gaza suffer siege, humanitarian crisis and recurring bouts of deadly violence.

There has always been Palestinian resistance to the apartheid, racism and violence of the Israeli state. That resistance continues. So, too, does the global movement of solidarity – a movement that is simultaneously anti-colonial, anti-war and anti-racist. It is a popular movement from below, just as the most hopeful Palestinian resistance is the popular struggle that provides a counterpoint to the Palestinian Authority's complicity in apartheid.

Ultimately, a single secular and democratic state – respecting the rights of Palestinians and Jews alike – is required across the whole of Palestine. Only such an alternative can fulfil the rights, aspirations and needs of all the Palestinian people.

Can we avert climate chaos and meet people's needs?

Feyzi Ismail

The capitalist system is driving us towards climate chaos and at the same time failing to meet people's needs. This is because, in the pursuit of endless economic growth, it is based on blind competition between corporations and countries, and maximising profits by pushing down wages. Capitalist expansion requires overconsumption in order to maximise profits, which makes consumerism, planned obsolescence, and unsustainable business models unavoidable. This occurs alongside underconsumption; an inability for vast swathes of the global population to meet even basic needs. Proposed solutions to these problems vary, from techno-utopianism to ethical consumerism, but both are limited unless they challenge the fundamental sources of the crisis: capitalist production and its exploitation of both labour and nature. Rather, as humanity stands perilously close to the edge of climate and ecological breakdown, what is urgently needed is a move towards more conscious planning.

Techno-utopian arguments focus on the power of technology to meet people's needs. At the extreme end, which includes versions of eco-modernism, the argument goes that people can continue to lead fossil-fuel-driven and hyper-consumerist lifestyles, while technology – such as various forms of geoengineering – will deal with the consequences. These technologies may very well be necessary in the future, given that we are already experiencing extreme climate events and are decades behind schedule in addressing the emergency. However, they are uncharted and evade the core of problem, which is the need to immediately halt investment in fossil fuels and switch to alternative energy sources. Relying on techno-fixes ignores the fact that technologies are not neutral but arise out of unequal social relations, and are shaped by those who control them. This reliance also fails to challenge the market logic of a production system that is built on fossil-fuel extraction, deforestation, agribusiness and other drivers of ecological crisis; practices which are the most profitable for companies.

A left-wing version of techno-utopianism argues that technological advances must be embraced because they mean abundant supply for all, and that what is needed is a social-democratic government that can distribute these resources in a more equitable manner. Such a government is certainly a starting point, and no radical Green New Deal will be put in place without one. What is discounted, however, is the fact that neither technology nor a social-democratic government will solve the underlying problem. If the capitalist system needs constant expansion in order for profits to be made – with a focus on GDP growth, the seeking out of new markets and so on – according to competitive principles, then this requires the relentless exploitation of people and of natural resources. Often this includes imperialist war. For people's needs to be genuinely met, popular democratic control over technology is essential, and that will require an overturning of capitalist social relations by working people.

In contrast, another set of arguments focus on ethical consumerism, which amounts to changing people's needs in the first place: people should consume less, become vegans, stop flying and watch their carbon footprints. Some people are already changing their lifestyles, but individual consumer choices designed to absorb the problems of capitalist production could never amount to the scale of change required. It also assumes that demand drives supply – that consumer choices determine what is produced – rather than the other way around, which is that companies produce what is profitable and ultimately shape consumption. Moreover, ethical consumerism allows the corporations, whose production processes are the source of the vast majority of emissions, to be let off the hook entirely.

Concentrating efforts on either of these approaches neglects the causes of the crisis. The first defends overconsumption while the second places the burden of responsibility on individual action. In the process, both underestimate the scale of the crisis, absolve corporations and governments of culpability, including obligations to address the crisis, and allow the market to dictate the solutions. And if the sole focus of engaging the market in climate solutions is to consider the costs of addressing the crisis, weighed against costs to the global economy, this fails to grasp the costs of potential societal and civilisational breakdown.

Far from counterposing the tasks of averting climate chaos and meeting people's needs, it is vital that they are addressed simultaneously. A radical Green New Deal that prioritises and recognises the value of jobs in welfare – health, education and other caring industries – repurposes polluting industries into sites of clean energy production, and even carbon capture and storage, for example, while establishing the foundations for democratic control of production, is an important start. It would begin the process of challenging the ultimate driver of the climate and ecological emergency – a system of production driven by a capitalist class that prioritises profit above all else.

How can a radical Green New Deal be achieved, even under a right-wing government? We need a mass movement that can fight for at least elements of a Green New Deal in the immediate term. This means building movements against the climate crisis but also, and perhaps more importantly, against imperialist war, austerity, and exploitative working conditions: movements that can help bring down right-wing governments. No progressive government that replaces the right will be kept in place without a mass movement. Whichever government is in power, organising towards these ends needs to happen in the here and now.

Why is there never enough money for the NHS?

Alia Butt

It seems that we're constantly being told that the NHS is unaffordable and that our healthcare demands keep growing beyond what a public service can sustain. This is the established story, but is it the reality? In actual fact, the UK spend per person on healthcare is lower than that of countries like France or Germany, and less than half that of the US. Our spend on long-term care is also lower than that of most other First World nations. So, why the insistence that the NHS is unreasonably expensive?

The truth about the NHS is that the private sector has been enmeshed within it from the very beginning. When the Labour government that was elected after World War Two moved to set up a national health service, the overwhelming majority of doctors, including the BMA, were vehemently opposed. The Tories voted against the bill twenty-one times. The NHS that resulted was a compromise, with GP surgeries remaining as private businesses and senior doctors allowed to continue their private practices.

The uneasy co-existence of the public sector and the private sector in the health service continues to this day with the balance tipping further in favour of private ownership. The drive towards privatisation started almost immediately with the introduction of prescription charges in 1952. Politicians ideologically opposed to the NHS as a public service have never wanted us to see free healthcare as possible. They prefer we understand the NHS as something needing private-sector 'efficiencies' to function effectively.

In 1983, for example, Thatcher deceitfully promised to keep the NHS safe, but was keen to underline how much public money it took: 'Let us never forget this fundamental truth: the state has no source of money other than the money that people earn themselves .... People talk about a free service. It isn't free. You have to pay for it.' Thatcher's complaint here was that the wealthy and corporations were having to pay their share of everyone's healthcare costs, as opposed to a private model where everyone had to find the money to pay for their own healthcare needs, regardless of their capacity to do so.

It is the oldest trick in the book to destabilise a social infrastructure intentionally by taking more money out of it so it becomes completely inadequate and collapses under pressure. The more the government creates crises in the NHS, the more the potential support for privatisation, even from people who don't like the idea but agree that things are currently unsustainable.

Whether it be the winter crises, mental-health crisis, wheelchair crisis, bed crisis, cancer-care crisis, maternity crisis, emergency-service crisis; all have been generated and maintained by the conservative government's drive to syphon taxpayer money away from the NHS and into other areas of spending. The Covid19 crisis has indeed been a catalyst for the demise of the NHS, but the NHS would not have been at such a weakened starting point had it not been for over a decade of unnecessary austerity.

With unchallenged Tory corruption on the rise, privatisation is now thoroughly ripping through the NHS. Twenty-five percent of NHS funding is going into private companies. GP surgeries are increasingly in corporate hands, for example, and many people are resorting to the use of private healthcare as NHS waiting lists lengthen to record highs. Crucially however, much like before the creation of the NHS, many others once again go without.

The Health and Care Bill will mean further uncertainty. Legislation will make it easier for private companies to bid on tenders without competition, while allowing them to sit on boards that make decisions where and how taxpayer money is spent. It will also introduce a decrease in staff pay and deregulation of professions, leaving staff and patients to struggle further. The NHS will look less like the one imagined in 1948 - free at the point of use, delivered by well trained professionals – and more like the US system, which costs more than twice as much.

The private sector is keen on some kind of healthcare service as there is money to be made from it, but its involvement compromises equity, efficiency and affordability. The fairest and cheapest way to provide decent healthcare to all remains a publicly funded and publicly run health service.

Why is housing so expensive?

Reuben Bard-Rosenberg and Dominic Alexander

Housing has been a marked problem in capitalist society since the industrial revolution. In the nineteenth century, workers were condemned to poorly built 'back-to-backs', to single rooms for whole families, and even to living in flood prone coal-cellars beneath terraces. The development of council housing did something to ease these problems, and set some limits on exploitation by private landlords. The dismantling of council housing is therefore one major factor in the return to Victorian levels of crowding in parts of London, for example.

This historic pattern reveals the problem also of the typical explanation for the cost of housing, which is 'supply and demand'. This golden rule of the market just does not operate in the case of housing, where most people face a range of constraints about proximity to jobs and services, and are subject to the social power of employers and landlords. Moreover, as Marx pointed out for market relations in general, at the point of equilibrium, the 'law' of supply and demand explains nothing about price.

'Supply and Demand' doesn't operate as the driving factor in housing for a variety of reasons. Firstly, the demand side is a social need with significant constraints, but the supply is determined by the interests of capital. Housing isn't necessarily made available for consumption, in the way that food is, for example. It can be, and increasingly is, used as a capital investment, without regard for its use value as a shelter for people. In recent decades, when profitable investment has been increasingly scarce worldwide, putting money into real estate is a safe way to store surplus capital. Its social use is irrelevant, and is pushed aside.

For governments in the neoliberal era, the demands of capital outweigh the need for workers to have a place in which to live. This explains much about how policy responds to the increasing unaffordability of housing. The 'Help To Buy' scheme is only of use to very well paid professionals, who need to be kept on the side of capital. Its real purpose, however, is to help financial institutions that enable the 'property bubble' to sustain itself and expand.

During both the crash of 2008 and the pandemic, the London housing market wobbled a little and then prices kept on moving up. This is not an accident. The point of 'Help to Buy' was to sustain house prices in a crisis with a big injection of government backed finance. The government has a policy of not allowing house prices to drop in those core real-estate markets - such as London - which account for the majority of national real-estate wealth.

Whilst the government's permanent high-price policy benefits the buy-to-let investor class, influential within its parliamentary party, this is first and foremost about the banks. A huge amount of debt in the banking system is secured against real estate. That is to say, the key security the bank has if their debtors don't pay, is that they get to grab the property that the money was borrowed to buy. If real-estate prices fall, the banks face being unable to recoup what they lent, and the balance sheets of financial institutions begin to turn nasty. And to avert this we have a series of policies that amount to Keynesianism for Bankers.

This isn't just a question of London, or the policies of British governments, however; it is a world-wide phenomenon that in centres of capital, where real estate was already relatively expensive, it has become inflated to a point that it becomes a flashpoint in the crisis of the whole system, as became evident in 2008. This is due to the enormous overaccumulation of capital in a long period since the 1960s of falling rates of profit. It is further due to the tendency for capitalism to centralise in certain regions, leaving others adrift. After all, property prices in post-industrial towns and cities plummet as wealth concentrates in the financial hubs of different countries.

For decades it's been felt instinctively that house prices in the centres where jobs are more abundant can't simply keep on rising beyond what people can afford. Within this whole context, the often American-imported rhetoric about 'gentrification' can be a political cul-de-sac. The tendency here is to frame society - and real estate in particular - as a jostling for position amongst competing tribes of wage earners. People from Peckham, we are told, can't afford to live there 'because the hipsters have moved in'. This renders invisible the institutions, and forms of money power that truly dominate our lives. If we want housing justice, we need to turn our fire not just on the landlords and the banks, but on the logic of the system that prefers the good of capital to social need. We need to turn against the politics that makes profitability a non-negotiable fact of life.

Section 3: How do we get socialism?

Is revolution possible in the twenty-first century?

Katherine Connelly

Yes. We know this is true because there have been revolutions in the twenty-first century, for example the revolutions of the 'Arab Spring' in 2011 that overthrew dictatorships in Tunisia and Egypt.

The assumption behind this question is that the nineteenth-century world Karl Marx knew, of smoky factories where large groups of workers produce commodities, has been replaced by 'tech' and a service-sector economy – at this point someone usually mentions that some people even get to play ping pong or sit on beanbags at work! And, therefore, Marxist ideas are no longer relevant. This argument is very superficial.

It doesn't really describe the world of work today. When Marx was writing, the working class was only a tiny proportion of the world's population. Even in a capitalist country like France, the majority of the population were peasants living in the countryside. Now the working class is global and big multinational companies (maybe even with beanbags in their offices) run sweatshops across the global South. In Britain and the US, as the Covid-19 pandemic exposed, working people still labour together in large numbers: think of the outbreaks in meat-packing factories and indeed Amazon warehouses.

That the nature of much work has changed is nevertheless undoubtedly true, but this would have been the least surprising aspect of capitalism to Marx, who identified that it was an essentially and uniquely revolutionary economic system. It cannot be static, it needs to find new markets constantly, to 'increase productivity' (meaning profits), to reduce 'costs' (meaning our wages), and find new technological innovations to drive other capitalists out of the market and grab more for themselves.

Such innovations make capitalism a hugely productive system. This means that no one need go without a home, or healthcare, or food. But because capitalism is organised around profit and not human need, hundreds of millions of people do. For all its productive capacity, capitalism is also an essentially destructive system: wars and climate change are two devastating symptoms.

So, not only is there a need for a revolution in the twenty-first century in order to reorganise society to meet human needs, capitalism has also created the possibility for those needs to be met.

Capitalism is inherently unstable because it cannot get away from the contradiction at its heart: that it relies on the exploitation of the vast majority of people (workers) who are not paid the value of what they produce. Instead, a proportion is expropriated as profits before we even see our wage slip. This mechanism, essential to the survival of capitalism, is reliant upon the work of those who have no interest in perpetuating this system.

Although the establishment invests a lot of effort to make us feel disempowered and atomised there are times when people overwhelmingly reject reactionary ideas. Even before the Covid-19 crisis, there were a series of insurgent, mass struggles across the globe: in Iraq, Sudan, Lebanon, Algeria, Colombia, Chile and Ecuador.

Today, with a huge public-health crisis intensified by the relentless drive for profit and in the face of an imminent, severe economic crisis, people are taking to the streets and organising to demand a different kind of society. In these circumstances, revolutionary change looks more, not less, likely.

Revolutions have happened and will happen in the twenty-first century. The key question is whether they can be successful. That depends how well organised we are and upon the strength of socialist ideas that show how another world, organised by and for human beings, can be won.

Can economic planning work?
Dominic Alexander

For well over a generation, there has been a mainstream consensus that economic planning cannot work. This has ruled out even a discussion of socialism. Yet, it has not always been like this. After the Second World War, when all the warring states engaged in state-led planning, there was a widespread assumption that post-war economies would depend on planning for rebuilding.

In West Germany for example, the newly founded conservative party, the Christian Democratic Union, began with a working assumption that the capitalist market would have to be subordinated to social planning. Under US pressure, the Christian Democrats rowed back from this position, but West Germany always retained a high degree of government co-ordination of economic activity. So did post-war Japan and many other successful states.

A planned economy is entirely feasible today, because in many respects we already have one. The problem is that the planning is done by the great corporations for profit, rather than for social need or environmental sustainability. The idea that capitalism is based upon a mass of individual decision making, all resolved through the 'market', had some truth to it once. However, even by the mid-twentieth century, this model no longer applied.

The gigantic, multinational corporations which dominate today depend on sophisticated and elaborate planning across many different continents. Resources need to be sourced and transported, goods need to be manufactured using complex supply chains, and products need to be marketed and distributed for sale.

All of this involves planning. The problem is that the planning is done purely for the profit of a single corporation, which remains in competition with other capitalists, large and small. While cut-throat competition continues, the system has required the development of all the capabilities that would be needed to plan an economy for the social and environmental good.

This situation was tacitly accepted in the post-war period but that accepted version of reality was swept away by the resurgence of 'free-market' capitalism after the collapse of the command economies of the Soviet bloc in the early 1990s. The poor reputation of these economies has helped to banish the idea of planning from awareness as a current feature. They were seen to have been failures in comparison to Western capitalism, and to be undesirable options due to their highly oppressive nature. Two points need to be made here.

Firstly, it is a myth that the form of planned economy to be found in the Soviet Union and its satellites was a failure. In fact, the Russian economy was growing at a rate faster than the American in the post-war decades up to the global economic crisis of the 1970s.

Secondly, what brought it down as a system, apart from the strain of competing in an arms race with the US, was its authoritarian structure. Bottlenecks and wastage built up within the lines of production that were controlled rigidly from the centre. Stalinism was based on the exploitation of the working class, in a mirror-image of the Western system. As a result, it provoked resistance from below, and cynicism and corruption among those who ran it.

A planned economy does not have to take that form. It could be highly democratic involving local democratic planning, co-ordinated at higher levels by bodies that are also elected. Such a system could be geared towards social need and environmental sustainability, from the local to the global level. All the technology and the skills needed to make such a system already exist. It is a political question whether we are capable of creating the social power which could challenge the domination of capital and the drive of profit making.

Can socialism come through Parliament?

Morgan Daniels

Jeremy Corbyn's election as leader of the Labour Party in 2015 brought great hope. More than 300,000 people joined Labour as a result, inspired by a socialist with an impeccable record of fighting oppression, war, and austerity. Hundreds of thousands more heard Corbyn's message of change at rallies up and down Britain. Yet Corbynism would be defeated through a mix of relentless smears; sabotage at the top of the Parliamentary Labour Party; and a series of retreats and compromises, most damagingly over the European Union.

Was this defeat foretold? Is it impossible to achieve socialism through parliament? And what happens when left-wing governments are elected?

What is fundamental here is that the state is not some neutral entity which can be harnessed for alternately left or right-wing purposes, depending on who is in power. This is because it mostly comprises unelected bodies which are bent towards maintaining a capitalist status quo: the police, the army, the civil service, the Bank of England, MI5, the judiciary, the media, the House of Lords, and so on. The Labour Party itself is a key cog in the state, with a majority of its MPs committed to preserving capitalism.

The half-decade of Corbynism taught us precisely what the state thinks about the idea of an anti-war, anti-austerity government. Civil servants briefed the press on Jeremy Corbyn's unsuitability as leader. The media went into hyper drive, churning out endless lies about Corbyn as a person and ridiculing his fantastical socialist principles. A military general warned of a mutiny in the army if Labour won a general election, whilst British soldiers used a photo of Corbyn for 'target practice'.

The full weight of the state bears down on left-wing governments that do win elections. Harold Wilson's Labour, for instance, was elected on a radical ticket in 1974, pledging to bring about a 'fundamental and irreversible shift in the balance of power in favour of working people'. These plans were met sharply by all sorts of stately shenanigans. MI5 leaked intelligence about senior Labour politicians to the papers. The civil service stymied plans for nationalisation. Bankers led multiple runs on the pound. By the end of the 1970s, Labour was implementing harsh austerity policies.

All this was deployed against Labour governments or leaderships that were simply attempting to make the existing system fairer. Given the obstacles, even these attempts at radical reform could only have been pushed through with massive mobilisation of working people on the ground. The socialist project of democratising the economy and ending big business's stranglehold over society will require much higher levels of popular participation. It can only plausibly be achieved by a revolutionary movement from below.

None of this means that we should ignore progressive currents within parliamentary politics. A Corbyn-led government would likely have delivered significant improvements in the lives of the working class and given enormous confidence to activists up and down the country, and even internationally. It would certainly have put the question of fundamental change on the agenda. For these reasons the Corbyn project received continued support from socialists outside of the Labour Party.

It is important though that we draw some conclusions from the fact that even that prospect was too much for those who hold power in modern capitalist society. While Parliament remains important as a political forum, we mustn't fall into the trap of thinking that politics is confined to Westminster. Every strike, every protest, every popular campaign is intensely political and opens up the prospect of a much more participatory form of mass politics that can generate movements with massive power. The Left needs to focus on how popular resistance can be transformed into a force for fundamental change.

Why does the Labour party fail?

Alex Snowdon

The Labour Party has, for the last century, been a focus for working-class people's aspirations to improve society and achieve a fairer, more equal state of affairs for the great majority. It has also been - in office - a repeated source of disappointment and failure.

Labour is very different to the Conservative Party. The Tories represent the interests of the ruling class. Labour, by contrast, gives at least a distorted reflection of working-class interests and aspirations. As the name suggests, it was established to give a political voice to workers (and their families).

The gradual extension of the franchise - so that by 1928 all women and men aged 21 or above could vote - ensured that elections became a key arena of working-class struggle. Labour emerged as a political break from the Liberals, seeking to give an independent voice to the working class instead of tailing a ruling-class party. It had close connections with the trade unions.

Labour, however, has always balanced between representing working-class people and the pressures of capitalist society and the nation state. This is a characteristic of reformist, or social-democratic, parties internationally. There is a constant tension between class and nation. The 'national interest' in reality means reinforcing a status quo that benefits the rich and powerful.

Labour has often promised much in opposition and delivered little in office. Once in government, it prioritises the needs of managing the British state and pursues the 'national interest'. The pressures of British and international capitalism have been brought to bear on Labour governments when they have tried to deliver real reforms and challenge the power of capital. Almost always, Labour in office has caved in to such pressures: its right wing doing so with little reluctance, while the socialist minority is dragged along behind.

At times of economic boom, as after the Second World War, Labour has had space to enact reforms and improvements like building social housing, creating the NHS, and nationalising industries. Even at these times there has been a desire to avoid antagonising the capitalists. The reforming government of 1945, for example, limited the scope of nationalisation (the majority of industry remained in private hands), avoided anything resembling workers' control and provided vast compensation to the previous private owners.

At times of crisis for the system, Labour has been even weaker. In the late 1970s, Labour capitulated to demands from the International Monetary Fund to impose public-spending cuts. Unemployment was allowed to rise. 'Nation' took precedence over class. In effect, the ruling class was protected while the working class was made to pay.

In foreign policy, Labour has always propped up a cross-party consensus with the Tories. Since 1945 this has involved subordinating Britain to US imperialism. Tony Blair leading Britain into catastrophic wars in Afghanistan and Iraq was appalling, but largely in keeping with Labour's historic role in world affairs. The Washington consensus has dominated, including when Labour has been in opposition. Even during Jeremy Corbyn's time as party leader, there was massive resistance to shifting foreign policy leftwards.

Labour will continue to attract support from those who want to kick back against the Tories and alleviate the worst elements of neoliberal capitalism. It will also continue to be a source of bitter disappointment. Jeremy Corbyn's leadership inspired hope that Labour could become a more combative left-wing party, but Keir Starmer has clearly indicated that the Corbyn project is over. The Right is back in control.

Socialists need a clear understanding of the limits of Labour and, equally, of the need for independent organising through extra-parliamentary movements. We also need radical socialist organisation that is rooted practically in the struggles that take place in workplaces and on the streets.

How do we get fighting trade unions?

Unjum Mirza

The recent marked uptick of workers' struggles over safety, against fire and rehire, job cuts and attacks on pay, working conditions and pensions has presented real possibilities for socialists. From struggles for safe workplaces to the struggles against an employers' offensive aimed at making workers pay for the cost of the pandemic, millions have understood this simple truth: trade unions are the basic defence mechanism of the working class.

Capitalist production for profit is based on a framework of exploitative relations between the state, bosses and workers. The strength of trade unions lies in their ability to organise and mobilise the widest possible sections of the working class against that exploitation. Any socialist at work worth their salt should be a member, building and strengthening trade-union organisation.

But, trade unions are contradictory organisations. While trade unions act, in Marx's words, as 'centres of resistance against the encroachments of capital', that resistance is confined to improving the terms of labour *within* the framework of capitalist exploitation. Furthermore, as the name *trade* unionism suggests, unions bargain with employers to further the interests of *their* members not the interests of the *whole* class.

It was concomitant with the rise of large-scale and stable unions that a distinctly conservative layer of full-time officials rose to prominence within the trade-union movement. These trade-union bureaucracies balance between the state, employers and workers negotiating the terms of our exploitation under capitalism, often acting as managers of discontent. They exist in a state of compromise with the system.

Unlike the workers they represent, they enjoy better conditions, pay and material benefits received from the union, not from an employer. Their professional role and often social familiarity with employers and government ministers places them in a different social environment from the bulk of their members. Often, the preservation of the union becomes an 'end in itself' (Rosa Luxemburg).

While the root of the power of the trade-union bureaucracies lies in the membership - the mass of whom, most of the time, are not engaged in the affairs of the union - their role as a layer of professional officials acting as an intermediary between capital and labour lies at the root of their classic tendency to vacillate. They are in conflict with workers while at the same time, dependent on members; they avoid, circumvent or contain struggles, but are careful not to push collaboration with the state and employers so far as to appear impotent, and so they ensure workers' pressures are reflected to some extent.

Trade unions are therefore subject to contradictory pressures. On the one hand, employers' attacks on jobs, pay and conditions *push* workers toward collective organisation and action. On the other hand, the trade unions' strength in organising the widest class-wide unity also reveals an uneven consciousness and the *pull* of conservatism among some members. This encourages union leaderships to reach compromise with the employer sooner rather than later, in order to resolve disputes. Trade-union officials balance between different sections of the unions' own memberships, often playing toward the lowest common denominator to maintain unity while keeping in check the more active and rebellious sections in the union by relying on those who are more passive.

Many trade unions and union officials are affiliated to, or are members of, the Labour Party. A divide between a union's 'economic' and 'political' spheres of activity and influence is encouraged. The Labour Party is a reformist organisation that seeks compromise with the capitalist system, which in turn reinforces the conservatism of the trade-union bureaucracy. When out of government, the Labour Party seeks to appear 'responsible' and 'fit to govern' exerting pressure on trade-union officials to reign in any militancy that may harm its electoral prospects. When in government, the Labour Party exerts even greater pressure on trade-union officials to compromise while they manage capitalism in the interests of those who wield real power; the unelected boards of corporations, employers and the state.

But the trade-union bureaucracy is not homogenous. Trade-union officials do hold differing ideological and political positions with real significance between *left* and *right* officials. Socialists are not neutral on the question: we have a vested interest in opposing the right. However, how left officials behave and act depends on the *specific circumstances*. In periods of low struggle they behave one way and sometimes can even appear to the left of the rank and file. In periods of high struggle and radicalisation, their conservatism comes to the fore, even while under pressure from below. In the final analysis and particularly at times of great radicalisation and inter-sectional struggle, the differences between left and right-wing officials are *secondary* to the fact that they belong to a conservative social stratum. Most importantly, the difference between left and right officials is *subordinate* to the *fundamental* antagonism between the union bureaucracy and the rank and file.

As socialists, our strategic orientation is to the base of the unions - the rank and file - because it is here that our activity, initiatives, newsletters, meetings, etc. bring together ordinary workers and reps and where we are best positioned to forge alternative sources of leadership to the conservative pressure of the full-time officials. It is among the rank and file that we spread the solidarity for striking workers within and across industries, maximising the confidence, combativity and consciousness of workers to organise and fight, while minimising the influence of officials who wish to dampen the struggle.

We stand in the tradition of the rank-and-file organisation, the Clyde Workers Committee, which summed up the right attitude towards the trade-union leaders in November 1915: 'We will support the officials just so long as they rightly represent the workers, but we will act independently immediately they misrepresent them.'

As socialists we argue that the emancipation of the working class can only be the act of the working class. That cannot be realised through compromise and accommodation with capitalism. It can only be realised through socialist revolution and the destruction of the capitalist state. That is why, for any conscious, socialist political minority, it is also necessary to maintain its own *independent* organisation, within the unions and any rank-and-file organisation it helps build.

Should socialists support the break-up of Britain?

Chris Bambery

The British state today is visibly in crisis. While the Scottish National Party was one seat short of an overall majority in the Scottish elections, there is still a clear majority for pro-independence parties in the Scottish Parliament.

The SNP promises an independence referendum again next year, riding high on polls showing majorities for independence since summer 2020. This is opposed by leading Westminster politicians including Prime Minister Boris Johnson and the Labour Leader Keir Starmer. Meanwhile, Johnson's Brexit deal has effectively left Northern Ireland in the EU and created a border with the rest of the UK, triggering the possibility of a referendum on Irish re-unification.

Socialists should surely defy Westminster and champion the right of Northern Ireland and Scotland to leave Britain as a matter of democratic principle.

World capitalism historically developed unevenly and involved the oppression of most nations by a handful of powerful and developed imperialist states. These denied the others even the most basic form of self-rule: the right to establish their own state.

Socialists developed an approach of supporting national movements which destabilise the imperialist system and weaken the ruling classes, while championing the international unity of the working class. Such reasoning is evident in the attitudes of Karl Marx and Friedrich Engels towards the world's oldest capitalist state, Britain.

Britain was inextricably linked to Empire and the oppression of Ireland from its beginnings. After King

James took the English and Scottish crowns in 1604, there was an acceleration of the Protestant colonisation of Ireland at the expense of the native population, especially in the 'Plantation of Ulster'. Catholics were treated as second-class citizens by Protestant settlers, and Ireland was prevented from developing economically. Moreover, in the 1840s, more than a million Irish people starved to death while Britain continued to take Irish grain.

Rather than benefit English workers, this situation weakened them. As Marx put it, observing the attitudes of English workers to Irish migrants working in British industry: 'In relation to the Irish worker [the English worker] regards himself as a member of the ruling nation and consequently he becomes a tool of the English aristocrats and capitalists against Ireland, thus strengthening their domination over himself.' It was on this basis that Marx championed Irish independence, which remains incomplete even after Britain was forced to leave most of Ireland in the face of stiff resistance in 1921.

Scotland, unlike Ireland, was never an oppressed nation. Its ruling class was an equal partner in the venture of Empire. Scottish nationalism arose in response to imperial decline after the First World War. By the close of the twentieth century, Scotland began to lag behind. Most Scots blamed the Tories, but Labour repeatedly failed to reverse the trend, even after championing devolution in the 1990s. Tony Blair's neoliberal policies and the Iraq War were widely seen as betrayal. No wonder Labour lost control of Scotland in 2007. No wonder it became Scotland's third party after teaming up with the Tories to see off independence in 2014.

For socialists, Scottish independence is about breaking Britain's imperial power. It is about crippling the British Army, which disproportionately recruits in Scotland. It is about paralysing Trident: moving Britain's nuclear-weapons system out of Scotland would be highly expensive and logistically difficult. And it is about derailing Britain's so-called special relationship with the US and thereby weakening Nato.

English workers would stand to gain as their ruling class would be in disarray. Meanwhile, Scottish workers would face a struggle from day one of independence against their new rulers in Holyrood.

Does a biased media make change impossible?

Des Freedman

For some time, people have been arguing that the internet would diversify the voices on offer in the media. Yet the same groups that dominated the old media now dominate online: the *Sun, Guardian, Mail, Telegraph, Independent, Express* and *Mirror* all reach tens of millions every month. Meanwhile, during the pandemic, the BBC's TV news bulletins were watched by over twenty million people. We still have a media system dominated by offshore billionaires and unaccountable elites with an entrenched hostility to radical ideas and movements.

These are the media organisations who vilified Jeremy Corbyn, ridicule any systematic attempt to redistribute wealth, and tend to back UK foreign policy because, apparently, it's in the 'national interest'. They may not tell us exactly what to think but, as the political scientist Bernard Cohen once put it, 'they tell us what to think about'.

This matters because the constant stream of 'official sources' and pro-austerity and anti-immigrant arguments is bound to have an impact. The people who run the media certainly think they are influential. Straight after the Brexit referendum, the *Sun*'s editor commented: 'So much for the waning power of newspapers.'

How then can we expect millions of voters to reject ruling-class arguments and instead embrace progressive and anti-establishment ideas?

The first thing to say is that audiences are not simply 'brainwashed' by what they consume. You can tell because polls on almost all issues show audiences are consistently to the left of the media. That's why despite the onslaught against Jeremy Corbyn, Labour won nearly thirteen million votes in 2017 and over ten million votes in 2019.

This is because people make their minds up according to their experience of life more than from the ideas they get in the education system or from the media. As Marx put it: 'Consciousness does not determine life. Life determines consciousness.' If your experience is one of insecurity, low wages, lack of opportunities and police brutality, then you're less likely to agree with a media that has promoted the benefits of a free market. It's not that surprising, in this context, that the British press is the least trusted across Europe.

Secondly, the power of media messaging is fundamentally affected by what goes on in the world around us. Mass movements like the great anti-war struggles, anti-austerity campaigns and the Black Lives Matter protests affect the views of all those who take part in them, and when they are big enough, force themselves onto the media's agenda. Once people are involved in collective struggle, we are far less likely to believe what we consume in mainstream media.

Genuinely national or international struggles can win the battle of ideas in wider society. The anti-war movement over Iraq, for example, helped convince the overwhelming majority in Britain and many other countries that the war was wrong, despite the fact that most of the media supported it.

Historically, great revolutionary movements go further and challenge all the preconceptions in society. In the Russian Revolution of 1917, in Spain in 1936 or the French events of 1968, people's ideas were turned upside down, all forms of oppression were challenged, and working people started to take over society for themselves, bringing into question the very idea of class rule. In these circumstances the movement's media becomes dominant and workers start to take over the old media institutions themselves. This is what Marx meant when he said that 'in the process of changing the world, we change ourselves.'

Will technology save us?
Elaine Graham-Leigh

There is an argument that we will be liberated from capitalism by new forms of technology. The theory here is that modern technological developments will prove to be fundamentally incompatible with capitalism.

Sometimes this is about information technology. In this view, the way that the internet has developed to enable people to collaborate with each other, in maintaining Wikipedia or creating open-source software, for example, creates peer-to-peer networks which don't depend on the market. More recent developments like blockchain will accentuate this, so that, as this argument goes, whether it is by organising a local co-op or using cryptocurrency, more and more people would be able to operate outside capitalist market structures and state control.

The other main version of this argument, in contrast, sees the liberating technology as improvements in production, including AI, which will make production so cheap that it will usher in an age of 'extreme supply' in which most things are so cheap they can just be given away.

Neither of these arguments take proper account of how capitalism has successfully used new technology to reproduce itself in the past, and demonstrably continues to do so. In their different ways, both of these predictions of the future envisage capitalism being hollowed out from within. The structures of the markets would still be there, but increasingly people would be living outside them for many aspects of their lives. In the end, presumably, capitalism would simply wither away from lack of use. In this scenario, there's little use for revolutionary organising.

Lenin and Trotsky, in this view, were writing for workers on different technology in a different age, so have little to offer us in the twenty-first century.

In many ways, things would be easier if we could just sit back and let blockchain liberate us, but is this really how it works? It is clear from the history of the last few centuries that new technologies can make profound differences to people's lives, whether for good or ill (and sometimes both). That isn't the same, though, as an argument that the technology itself causes social changes, still less a change in the system itself.

We often think of capitalism as being synonymous with the technologies of the Industrial Revolution, in particular the wide-scale use of fossil fuels. The reality, though, is that capitalism as a mode of production predates the Industrial Revolution. Capitalism's unique inherent tendency for environmental destruction is evident in its early form, as can be seen in various places as early as the seventeenth century.

It is not of course that there is no relationship between the types of technology in use and the economic, political and social system. The huge increases in productive power that fossil fuels allowed were fundamental to capitalist profitability, so it's not as if the Industrial Revolution was a random event, unrelated to the development of capitalism. The point though is that this isn't a simple relationship. We can't boil it down to 'burn coal, get capitalism.' Nor is the way out of the current system as simple as 'stop burning coal, stop capitalism.'

Capitalism is a dynamic system, which as we know has driven and survived huge changes in technology in a short space of time. These technological developments aren't random but are produced by capitalist competition and capitalism's need for growth and expansion into new areas. Think, for example, of the way in which social networks have effectively commodified our personal networks.

This isn't to argue that we shouldn't use modern

technology where it's helpful for the struggle. What we have to understand, though, is that it provides means and platforms for organising; it doesn't take the place of organisation. The task of building a movement to fight back against exploitation and oppression is the same in essentials whether you're building the Peasants' Revolt of 1381 by walking from village to village, or organising a People's Assembly demonstration in 2021 through Zoom meetings and WhatsApp chats.

There is no piece of technology or general technological development which will automatically make capitalism redundant. We live in a world which is technologically very different from that of, say, Russia in 1917, but the lessons of past proletarian struggles are still very relevant to us today.

How should socialists organise?

Dragan Plavšić

Socialists need to be organised because the ruling class is. Not to be organised guarantees defeat at the hands of those who are. This much is uncontroversial. So, the key question becomes how best to organise to defeat our opponents and bring about socialism.

Two different models of organising are usually advanced here, and they are rooted in the different world-views of reformists and revolutionaries.

Reformists argue in favour of winning incremental reforms within the limits of capitalist society. Some who still use the word 'socialism' maintain that reforms will edge us towards it. Reformists thus believe in working within capitalist institutions like parliament and the state to pass reforms. Their focus is fighting and winning elections and forming governments, which is why reformist parties are so passive between elections.

As a result, electoralism comes to determine the character of reformist political parties. They are broad parties that cast their nets far and wide over the working class (and beyond), regardless of the uneven and contradictory views people hold, in order to attract as many votes as possible. This is why, for fear of losing votes, reformist parties like the Labour Party are drawn as if magnetically to the political middle ground, though what really anchors them there is their ideological starting-off point: their commitment to working within the limits of capitalist society.

By contrast, revolutionaries argue that socialism can never be achieved by merely winning reforms within these limits. On the contrary, it is the cracks in these limits that need to be exploited in order to overturn capitalist society as a whole.

As a result, this different goal necessitates a political party with a different character, a revolutionary party made up of militant workers. Instead of a broad party adapting itself to the uneven consciousness of workers for the sake of votes, a revolutionary party seeks to overcome this unevenness by organising militant workers capable of giving a lead in the class struggle.

A revolutionary party of this kind can only be effective, however, if it is wedded to the democratic principle Marx and Engels expounded, that 'the emancipation of the working class must be the act of the working class itself.' This entails building a party embedded in the working class, so that its militants are best placed to raise the consciousness of the class against the limits of capitalist society.

None of this means ignoring elections, but it does mean they are not the focus of a revolutionary party. Instead, its focus is on extra-parliamentary agitation for reforms, on demonstrations, on strikes, in social and anti-war movements with the potential to raise the conscious combativity of the working class. Whenever possible, this means linking arms with reformists to advance the class struggle.

Because reformist parties cast their nets wide for electoral purposes, people on the left are most likely to join them, accounting for the large memberships which are their greatest asset. But size cannot overcome their fatal flaw; that they are designed to seek reform within the limits of capitalist society but not to bring about socialism. Indeed, especially in neoliberal times, respecting the limits of capitalist society has been altogether more important for reformist parties than reforms for the working class. As a result, their support has tended to wane.

By contrast, although the revolutionary approach is

more daunting, its critical advantage is its clear-sighted understanding that reformist parties have not brought us closer to socialism because this is not in fact their purpose. Thus, we need a different organisation, a revolutionary party of militants specifically designed to overturn capitalism and bring about socialism.

Thanks are due to the members of the Counterfire publications group – Morgan Daniels, Feyzi Ismail, Dragan Plavšić and Alex Snowdon – for their work in seeing this project through to publication, and to Chris Nineham, who started the whole thing off on the website. Many thanks also to Neil Darby for the design and layout and, of course, last but not least, to all the contributors who made this book possible.

Elaine Graham-Leigh